MAD about

GYMNASTICS

JUDITH HENEGHAN

WAYLAND

WAYLAND

First published in 2015 by Wayland
Copyright © Wayland 2015

Wayland
338 Euston Road
London NW1 3BH

Wayland Australia
Level 17/207 Kent Street
Sydney, NSW 2000

Editor: Nicola Edwards
Design: Rocket Design (East Anglia) Ltd

A catalogue record for this title is available
from the British Library.

ISBN: 978 0 7502 8270 3
Library e-book ISBN: 978 0 7502 8840 8
Dewey number: 796.4'4-dc23

Printed in China

Wayland is a division of
Hachette Children's Books,
an Hachette UK company

The author and publisher would like to thank the following for allowing their pictures to be reproduced in this publication: Cover: all Shutterstock; p4 (t) Shutterstock.com/Kyle Lee, (b) Shutterstock.com/Lissandra Melo; p5 (t) Shutterstock.com/Galina Barskaya, (b) Shutterstock.com/dotshock; p6 (t) Shutterstock.com/Monkey Business Images, (b) Shutterstock.com/mimagephotography; p7 (t) Shutterstock.com/Ianych, (b) Shutterstock.com/holbox; p8 Getty Images; p9 (t) Getty Images, (b) Peter Read Miller/Sports Illustrated/Getty Images; p10 (t) Andy Cross/The Denver Post via Getty Images, (b) Anthony Devlin/PA Wire; p11 (t) Featurefash/Shutterstock.com, (b) Alexander Hassenstein/Bongarts/Getty Images ; p12 (t) Getty Images (DAJ), (b) Shutterstock.com/ Paolo Bona; p13 (t) Shutterstock.com/ Sasha Samaerdzija; (b) Wikimedia Commons; p14 (t) Shutterstock.com/ Michael C Gray, (b) Art Widak/Demotix/Demotix/Press Association Images; p15 Al Tielemans /Sports Illustrated/Getty Images; p16 Getty Images; p17 (t) FREDERIC J. BROWN/AFP/Getty Images, (m) Shutterstock.com/Galina Barskaya, (b) Shutterstock.com/Air Images; p18 (t) Shutterstock.com/roibu, (m) Shutterstock.com/bikeriderlondon, (b) Shutterstock.com/ITALO; p19 (t) John Thys/AFP/Getty Images, (b) Getty Images; p20 Shutterstock.com/Lilyana Vynogradova; p21 (t) Shutterstock.com/Lilyana Vynogradova, (b) Atsushi Tomura/Getty Images; p22 (t) Matthew J. Lee/The Boston Globe via Getty Images, (b) Shutterstock.com/Lilyana Vynogradova; p23 (t) BEN STANSALL/AFP/GettyImages, (b) Shutterstock.com/ Alexey Fursov; p24 (t) www.mentalfloss.com, (b) Shutterstock.com/Jacek Chabraszewski; p25 Miles Willis/Getty Images for Cirque du Soleil; p26 (t) Shutterstock.com/waldru, (b) Shutterstock.com/ John Lumb; p27 (t) Matt Dunham/AP/Press Association Images, (b) Tony Marshall/EMPICS Sport; p28 (t) Shutterstock.com/ alexkatkov, (b) Shutterstock.com/Jenella; p29 (t) Shutterstock.com/Michael C Gray, (b) Shutterstock.com/lev radin

Every effort has been made to trace the copyright holders. We apologise in advance for any unintentional omissions and would be pleased to insert the appropriate acknowledgements in any future editions of this publication.

Contents

Getting started

I'm totally mad about gymnastics! Jumping and tumbling give me a real buzz and I've always loved doing handstands, forward rolls and cartwheels. All I need is some space and a mat for soft landings. Last year I joined a club where I can build on my basic skills and learn some new ones.

All-round exercise

Gymnastics is an indoor sport that develops your agility, balance, strength and coordination. It is great for all-round fitness. The Ancient Greeks first developed it as a series of disciplined training exercises for competitors in public games. However, male and female circus performers and acrobats have also practised tumbling indoors and outdoors along with other physical feats for hundreds of years.

Different equipment

Gymnasts use a set range of equipment: floor, vault, beam, bars, rings and pommel horse. Rhythmic gymnasts use balls, ribbons or hoops, while pairs or teams of gymnasts may use each other's bodies for lifts, balances and jumps. Trampolining is also a form of gymnastics, with extra bounce! You can find out about all these different skills as you read this book.

A gymnast on the pommel horse.

top tip

The handstand is a basic position in all types of gymnastics — sooner or later you're going to need to balance upside down! Start by practising against a wall, with a gym mat underneath you. Stretch your toes up to the ceiling and keep your arms straight. Get used to how this feels before trying it without the wall to support you.

Once you've practised this, try doing a handstand away from the wall but make sure someone is standing by to hold your feet if necessary.

Warm up

I try to look after my body. Gymnastics is a strenuous sport so warming up is really important if I want to avoid injury, increase flexibility and help my muscles develop properly. My body needs to recover afterwards, too. I make time to cool down and rest. There's no point in rushing it!

Gently does it

Start every warm up with some gentle jogging or skipping on the spot. This increases your heart rate which allows your blood to pump faster and deliver more oxygen to the muscles that are going to be working hard as you stretch them. It also helps you 'loosen up' and release any tension.

This sh... ...up the

Stretching

Next, aim to stretch all the major muscles in your body, particularly those in your neck, shoulders, back and legs. Your instructor will show you the different stretches. A good stretch should feel a little tight to begin with, but it shouldn't be painful. To make sure your muscles get the most benefit, try to hold each stretch for a count of ten before you release it. You'll probably find you can push into the stretch a little more each time you do it.

top ☆ tip

Don't feel frustrated if you can't do a stretch like the bridge stretch straight away. If you practise every day, you'll soon find it gets easier. Your muscles will develop, your balance will improve and your confidence will grow, too!

Join a club

My local gymnastics club is my favourite place. I've been going for less than a year but I've made loads of friends there. We use the equipment and learn new skills from fully trained teachers. My teacher says I'm making great progress. I've already got a place in the junior squad and I've taken part in several competitions. They're really exciting!

Competing

Most gymnastic competitions are organised through clubs. There are different sorts of competitive gymnastics, including artistic, acro, rhythmic and trampolining. Artistic is the most popular — it includes floor, vault, bars, rings, beam and pommel horse. Competitors are judged in two ways: execution, which means how well the chosen routine is carried out, and degree of difficulty.

CHECKLIST

What to wear?

Gymnasts need to be able to move freely in every direction. Toes have to grip apparatus. The following are essential:

- ☑ Stretchy leotard for girls, shorts or leggings for boys;
- ☑ Bare feet or non-slip gym slippers;
- ☑ Hair out of eyes and tied back.

Everyone needs a coach

All gymnasts from beginners to Olympic medallists need a fully qualified instructor, or coach. It can be dangerous to try out new movements or use a piece of equipment on your own. Your coach will help you learn new skills safely, at the level that is just right for you. They are also there to support you in competitions and advise you about training. Always listen to your coach!

Always have a 'spotter' standing by whenever you practise a new move.

Artistic gymnastics

In artistic gymnastics, girls and boys compete separately, using different equipment. Women's artistic gymnastics includes the vault, floor, beam and asymmetric or uneven bars. Men's artistic gymnastics includes the vault, floor, pommel horse, rings, parallel bars and high bar.

THE EXPERT SAYS...

Practice makes perfect! Olympic gymnast Shawn Johnson (above) says: "I set daily, weekly and monthly goals that are challenging and attainable. It boosts my confidence."

Safe landing!

The first thing I learned at gym club was how to land safely. This means learning how to land on two feet, how to dismount from the beam, the vault and the bars, and how to do a safe recovery roll if I lose my balance. Knowing how to land safely has given me loads of confidence. I don't feel nervous about trying new things.

Regain your balance

A safe landing is where you land on two feet so that your weight is spread evenly. Knees should be bent a little to absorb the shock. Keep your back straight to protect your neck, and make sure your arms are stretched out in front of you to help you regain your balance. Gymnasts practise their landings all the time. In competitions, marks are deducted for a weak landing — for example, if the gymnast wobbles too much or forgets to keep their back straight.

The dismount is a vital part of any bar, vault or beam routine.

Mistakes are a big part of learning! Louis Smith, British Olympic silver-medallist, says: *"If I've fallen or if I've lost an event, it makes me want to work even harder. It makes me want to get even stronger to prove I can do it!"*

The safety roll

All gymnasts wobble, lose their balance and fall from time to time. When this happens, it may not be possible to land on two feet so it is important to practise the safe recovery roll. Keep your fists clenched, pull your arms in to your body and roll in the same direction as the fall. This helps reduce the impact of the fall.

top ★ tip

Practice makes perfect! Try a star jump and land in the safe landing position with your knees bent and your back straight. Keep practising until you can do it confidently without any wobbles.

Every gymnast should practise the safe recovery roll.

Vault

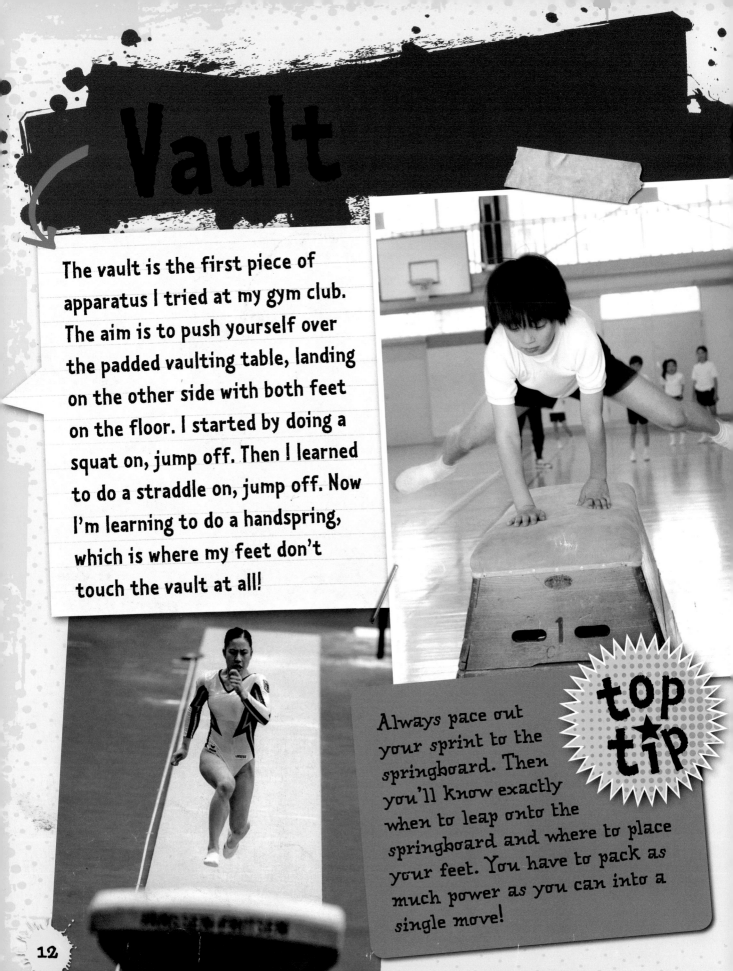

The vault is the first piece of apparatus I tried at my gym club. The aim is to push yourself over the padded vaulting table, landing on the other side with both feet on the floor. I started by doing a squat on, jump off. Then I learned to do a straddle on, jump off. Now I'm learning to do a handspring, which is where my feet don't touch the vault at all!

top tip

Always pace out your sprint to the springboard. Then you'll know exactly when to leap onto the springboard and where to place your feet. You have to pack as much power as you can into a single move!

The springboard take-off

The vault is really several pieces of equipment: a springboard, the padded vaulting table and safety mats on the other side. The springboard gives you the lift you need to get onto the vaulting table. It's important to run up to the springboard as fast as you can. A strong sprint will give you a powerful take off and help propel you through the air.

A simple handspring vault.

CHECKLIST

There are five stages to a vault, and they are all equally important.

- ☑ The run up to the springboard
- ☑ The jump from the springboard, called 'pre-flight'
- ☑ Contact with the vaulting table
- ☑ The time in the air before landing, called 'post-flight'
- ☑ Landing on two feet

The handspring

A handspring is where the gymnast takes off from the springboard and then flips in the air so that they land on the vaulting table on their hands. The hands then push off, propelling the gymnast upwards and over so that they land feet first on the safety mat. Once you have mastered the handspring, you can start to add extra twists and turns as you move through the air.

13

Floor

Floor is my favourite apparatus. I love the mix of acrobatic elements with artistic movements and gestures. It's really challenging though – you have just over a minute to incorporate lots of different balances, springs and jumps. In competitions you have to use the whole floor area, but you lose marks if you step outside the boundary!

England's Max Whitlock performs in the men's floor competition on his way to winning a gold medal at the 2014 Commonwealth Games in Glasgow.

Tumbling

Tumbling involves travelling in a straight line with a series of flips and handsprings. Gymnasts push off from feet to hands to feet and sometimes feet to feet. They are helped and supported by springs in the specially designed floor. The gymnast gains speed and power as the sequence builds. This is why a difficult move like a salto (a somersault in the air) usually comes at the end.

Girls and boys

Floor routines at competition level are up to 90 seconds long and usually contain several tumbling runs. However, the rules about floor are different for boys and girls. Girls' routines contain some dance elements, choreographed and set to music by the gymnast and her coach. They allow the gymnast to express her own personality. Boys' routines do not use music. They emphasise strength and acrobatic elements.

Female gymnasts use dance elements in their floor routines.

CHECKLIST

Make up a simple floor routine of your own, connecting the following elements with an elegant turn or graceful arm movements:

☑ Backward roll (keep your hands by your head to push off and back into the standing position)

☑ Cartwheel (keep your legs straight)

☑ Handstand (practise against a wall first)

☑ Forward roll (keep your head tucked in)

top tip

Keep your toes and fingers pointed during your routine. Not only does this look more elegant, it helps to strengthen your hands and feet.

Bars

The bars are the most fun to practise on. I couldn't wait to get started. It's all about swinging from your hands both above and below the bar. You use the power in the swing to do moves like handstands and saltos. You need strong shoulders and arms so we do loads of strengthening exercises on the floor before we mount the bars.

Getting started

Your gym club will have a special low training bar for you to learn some basic moves before you try them out on the high bars. Beginners learn to swing into a front support, which is an upright vertical body position with the arms locked and thighs touching the bar. From here you can swing your legs forwards, push your legs back and up into a handstand position, or bring your feet up onto the bar.

top tip

Always rub chalk on your hands and on the bars before you start, as this stops them getting slippery. Most gymnasts also wear wrist supports and special grips to protect themselves while swinging.

THE EXPERT SAYS...

Champion British gymnast Beth Tweddle knows how much practice it takes to become a world-class gymnast. Before competing at the 2012 Olympics she said: *"I will have trained 20 years for a 30-second bar routine, and a 90-second floor routine."*

Uneven and parallel bars

Girls compete on the uneven bars. They use the gliding swing to transfer their hands from one bar to the other, often in the splits position. Boys compete on the parallel bars and the high bar. The high bar is a single bar and male gymnasts use an all-round, full-circle swing to provide the power for exciting saltos and twists.

Doing the splits on the asymmetric bars.

Doing the splits

To do the splits, both your legs must be stretched out in opposite directions, to form one continuous line. It is a basic position in gymnastics, whether performed on the floor, on the beam or in the air. However, it takes a bit of practice. As with all stretches, don't attempt it without warming up first!

The balance beam

When I first went to gym club, the balance beam looked very high. Then my coach said that all beginners start on a low beam that rests on the floor. I didn't move up to the raised beam until I could jump and do a front walk-over without falling off. I still wobble sometimes, but the beam is padded which makes it less slippery and easier to grip with my fingers and toes.

The front walkover

The front walkover is a key movement on the balance beam. The gymnast bends forwards, places her hands on the beam and pushes off with her feet. She does the splits above her head and then brings her legs down, one after the other, to land on the beam behind her head. Now she can stand upright again. It takes quite a bit of practice, because you can't see where your feet are going!

Competition level

Only girls compete on the balance beam. A full routine combines acrobatic elements such as walkovers and rolls, dance elements such as leaps, balance poses such as handstands, and a dismount. It usually lasts 90 seconds. The emphasis is on smooth, controlled, elegant movements rather than speed. You need excellent balance. Wobbles cost marks!

top tip

Get confident with your beam routine by marking out a line on the floor that *is* five metres long and 10 cm wide. Start with forward rolls, cartwheels and walkovers. Ask a friend to tell you if you move off the line. When this happens, begin again!

CHECKLIST

Judges look for:

- ☑ a graceful mount
- ☑ elegant hands
- ☑ pointed toes
- ☑ no wobble
- ☑ good height in jumps
- ☑ good split extensions
- ☑ a clean, confident dismount.

Always practise with a spotter close by to support you.

Pommel horse and rings

My friend Ryan is getting really good on the pommel horse. He's been practising all year. He says the top gymnasts make it look so easy! But anyone taking up either the pommel horse or the rings needs lots of shoulder strength because your arms support your body weight the whole time. This is why these two events are for boys only.

top ★ tip

What to wear?

For both the pommel horse and rings, boys often wear close-fitting leggings rather than shorts because shorts can get caught on the apparatus.

Pommel

A pommel horse looks a bit like a high padded bench. It has two handles, known as pommels, on the top for your hands to grip. The idea is to keep your arms straight and your legs circling and swinging continually. Younger boys can practise leg circles and hand turns for the pommel horse on a 'mushroom', a piece of apparatus shaped like a mushroom with a rounded top.

The gymnast's legs can be together or apart but they must remain straight with toes pointed throughout the routine.

THE EXPERT SAYS...

World Champion Kohei Uchimura (right) says: "thoroughly enjoying a sport will help you become an Olympian".

Still rings

A routine on rings usually consists of swing, strength and hold positions. One of the most famous and difficult holds is known as the 'iron cross'. In this position, the gymnast must keep his arms perfectly horizontal and straight, while at the same time making sure the rings he's holding on to don't move about. It takes a huge amount of strength and poise!

Rhythmic style

Rhythmic gymnastics is really beautiful to watch. It uses more dance elements than artistic gymnastics and it's always performed on the floor, to music, using different kinds of hand-held apparatus. The balls, hoops and ribbons create gorgeous moving shapes. I'd love to try it!

The apparatus

There are five different kinds of hand apparatus in rhythmic gymnastics: hoops, ribbons, rope, clubs and balls. The individual gymnast uses one kind at any one time and must demonstrate her skill in throwing, catching, spinning, twisting and balancing the items combined with gymnastic leaps, turns, stretches and walkovers.

Rhythmic gymnasts need excellent hand-eye coordination.

THE EXPERT SAYS...

Evgenia Kanaeva (left) describes the training she does to be a rhythmic gymnastics world champion: "I train six days a week. From 8:30 am to 10 am I work with a choreographer to learn new routines. From 10 am to 1 pm I practise routines, then spend half an hour stretching and strength training, especially for my back and legs. After lunch, I return to the gym for a second training session with a one-hour stretching warm-up and two or three hours of practising routines."

Visual drama

Rhythmic gymnastics is graceful and poetic, with striking music, costumes and make-up to match. It interprets the music through highly athletic and flexible movement. Gymnasts compete as individuals or in teams of up to five members. Group work is especially dramatic as the gymnasts must perform in carefully choreographed time with each other and may use two kinds of apparatus at once.

top tip

The ball in rhythmic gymnastics should become a natural extension of the body, always in smooth, controlled motion. It can be supported by any part of the body, but if you use your hands, don't grasp or clutch it. Practise rolling the ball from your palm towards your shoulder and back again.

Acro

Acro stands for acrobatic gymnastics. It's a combination of traditional gymnastics and circus performance set to music and it's great if you like working with a partner or in a team. A tower of three or even four people looks really spectacular. The gymnast at the top needs a good head for heights!

A basic acro balance.

top tip

Remember, any balances or 'flighted' movement involving a partner should never be attempted on your own. You must be guided by a qualified instructor for the safety of both you and your partner.

A separate sport

Acro is a type of floor exercise that combines individual gymnastic skills with carefully constructed balances and 'flighted' throws and catches involving a partner or team member. Like rhythmic gymnastics, it is classed as a separate sport. Many acro techniques are used by performance groups such as Diversity, UK winners of Britain's Got Talent, and international acts like Cirque du Soleil.

Performers from Cirque du Soleil.

Different jobs

Each partner or team member has a different job to do. Those who hold up the other gymnasts are called bases. They need to be strong, muscular and steady. The 'top' gymnast must be light and agile in order to balance on the shoulders or head of someone else. Bases and tops need to trust each other completely, as many of the balances and throws require total dependence on each other.

CHECKLIST

Acro gymnasts compete in the following combinations:

- ☑ women's pairs
- ☑ mixed pairs (male base, female top)
- ☑ men's pairs
- ☑ women's trios
- ☑ men's fours.

Trampolining

All my friends love trampolining, whether they belong to a club or not! Jumping so high is a brilliant feeling, and great exercise too. But if you want to do more complicated moves, including somersaults and flips, you need to join a club. Like any sport, trampolining can cause injury without proper coaching.

Basic shapes

Each jump on the trampoline involves a basic shape. You can stay upright with your whole body vertical, or tuck your knees into your chest, or 'pike' which means bending your body at the hips to touch your toes while keeping your legs straight, or 'straddle' which means doing the same as for the pike but with feet apart. Once you have mastered these four basic shapes, you can add more complex turns and twists.

Pike in mid-air.

Landing positions

There are four main landing positions for safe landing on the trampoline. You can land on your feet, or your 'seat' (bottom), or on your front with your hands underneath your chin, or on your back in which case your arms and legs should be pointing upwards. It's really important to practise these basic techniques over and over again as they are the building blocks for any routine.

Bryony Page, British Trampolining Champion (right), says: *"I enjoy the feeling of being in the air. There is a point at the top of the jump where you feel weightless and feel like you can fly. You can go so high, there's so much variety. I really don't know why everyone doesn't do it!"*

THE EXPERT SAYS...

Gymtastic!

Gymnastics combines dance, acrobatics, speed, height, strength and balance. It uses every muscle from your fingers to your toes. I love everything about it – even the warm-ups! The feeling after achieving a new skill for the first time is fantastic. It keeps me smiling for days.

FreeG

FreeG is the name given to a new kind of freestyle gymnastics. It blends traditional gymnastics with martial arts kicks and the kind of leaps you see in parkour, or free-running. A number of clubs now offer classes in FreeG. You'll need to wear trainers and loose clothing rather than a traditional leotard or shorts. It's a more explosive style!

28

Skills and confidence

Whatever your style or favourite piece of equipment, gymnastics is an exhilarating sport that builds skills, confidence and friendships for life!

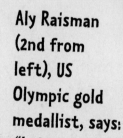

Just enjoy it – whatever your level!

top ★ tip

Gymnasts need energy as well as strong muscles and bones. Make sure you eat a balanced, varied diet with lots of fruit and vegetables. It's also important to stay hydrated at the gym so always drink plenty of fresh water.

THE EXPERT SAYS...

Aly Raisman (2nd from left), US Olympic gold medallist, says: "I think gymnastics is the best sport in the world, so just enjoy it. It's definitely very challenging, but that's what makes it so special and amazing. If you love it, the most important thing to remember is that anything is possible and to never give up."

Quiz

How mad about gymnastics are you? Try this quiz and find out!

1. What is the job of a spotter?

(a) the spotter looks for space for a gymnast to move in to;

(b) the spotter marks the spot on the floor where the gymnast needs to land;

(c) the spotter watches the gymnast and steps in to support their legs or back when needed.

2. Why do gymnasts rub chalk on their hands?

(a) to make their skin tougher;

(b) to increase grip;

(c) to mark the position of their hands on the bars or the beam.

3. What is a mushroom?

(a) a headstand with splits;

(b) a saggy leotard;

(c) a mushroom-shaped piece of apparatus for practising leg circles and hand turns.

4. In rhythmic gymnastics, what is the correct way to hold a ball?

(a) lightly balanced or cupped by any part of the body;

(b) grasped firmly in the hand;

(c) the ball should never touch the hands.

5. In acro, what is the job of the base gymnast?

(a) to do the most difficult part of the routine;

(b) to do the least acrobatic part of the routine;

(c) to support the top gymnast in an equal partnership built on mutual trust.

6. What is a pike?

(a) one leg forward, one leg behind;

(b) legs straight, feet together, bent at the hip so that legs and chest come closer together;

(c) a fishy dismount.

7. What happens if you step outside the boundary during a floor routine?

(a) you lose points;

(b) you are disqualified;

(c) nothing happens.

8. Why is it important to keep your back straight when you land?

(a) because you look more graceful;

(b) because this helps you land more accurately;

(c) because a straight back helps support your neck and protect it from injury.

Answers:
1(c); 2(b); 3(c); 4(a); 5(c); 6(b); 7(a); 8(c)

Glossary

acro the sport of acrobatic gymnastics, which is a partner/team sport.

apparatus a piece of equipment.

artistic gymnastics this includes vault, bars, rings, pommel horse, beam and floor.

base in rhythmic gymnastics, the gymnast who supports their partner gymnast.

beam an apparatus for girls only.

bridge stretch a key stretch with hands and feet on the floor, head facing outwards, and back arched to make a bridge shape.

choreographed where a sequence of movements is carefully designed.

dismount how a gymnast exits an apparatus such as the bars or beam.

execution how well a particular move or skill is carried out.

flighted movement in rhythmic gymnastics, where the base assists the top to move through the air.

floor a sprung area of floor for tumbling; a piece of apparatus.

freeG freestyle gymnastics.

handspring where the hands push off from the vaulting table to propel the body into the air.

high bar an apparatus for boys only.

mushroom an apparatus used in training for the pommel horse.

parallel bars two level bars; an apparatus for boys only.

pike where the body bends at the hips to bring the legs, straight and together, towards the body.

pommel horse an apparatus for boys only.

rhythmic gymnastics a type of gymnastics set to music, using hand-held apparatus such as a ball, hoop, ribbon or clubs.

safe recovery roll an important skill that helps protect the body in a fall.

salto a somersault in the air.

spotter someone who stands close to a gymnast, ready to support them when required.

springboard a sprung apparatus to help a gymnast mount the vaulting table or the beam.

squad gymnastics team.

still rings an apparatus for boys only.

top gymnast in acro, the gymnast who is lifted or supported by other gymnasts.

tumbling a sequence of rapid moves across the floor that might include cartwheels, walkovers, flips and saltos.

uneven bars also known as asymmetrical bars; an apparatus for girls only.

vault apparatus that includes the springboard and the vaulting table.

walkover a move from upright to a handstand with splits, continuing forward to upright again.

Index